To: Joyce & Gary — Christmas 2001
This year, at Christmas — someone is missing ... and I know how your heart aches for Jamie's presence. Take time to remember all the happy Christmas memories, and let them heal your heart. We'll always remember those that are gone from us — remember also those who love you so much!

Cindy & Brad

ISBN 1-58660-286-1
ISBN 1-58660-287-X

Cover photography © PhotoDisc, Inc.

Unless otherwise indicated, all Scripture quotations are taken from the HOLY BIBLE, NEW INTERNATIONAL VERSION®. NIV®. Copyright © 1973, 1978, 1984 by International Bible Society. Used by permission of Zondervan Publishing House. All rights reserved.

Scripture quotations marked KJV are taken from the King James Version of the Bible.

Scripture quotations marked RSV are from the Revised Standard Version of the Bible, copyright 1946, 1952, 1971 by the Division of Christian Education of the National Council of the Churches of Christ in the USA. Used by permission.

Scripture quotations from *The Message* © by Eugene H. Peterson 1993, 1994, 1995. Used by permission of NavPress Publishing Group.

Published by Barbour Publishing, Inc., P.O. Box 719, Uhrichsville, Ohio 44683
www.barbourbooks.com

Member of the
Evangelical Christian
Publishers Association

Printed in China.

With Deepest Sympathy

Marilou H. Flinkman

BARBOUR
PUBLISHING, INC.

I won't tell you not to cry.
Tears flow from the soul
to soothe your wounded heart.
Come, let me put my arms around you
and give you a shoulder to cry on.

Comfort

Do not feel awkward.
We are clumsy human beings
who, when grief stricken,
have permission to cry.
When Jesus came to Lazarus's tomb,
He wept.
He weeps with you now.

When Jesus therefore saw her weeping,
and the Jews also weeping which came with her,
he groaned in the spirit, and was troubled.
JOHN 11:33 KJV

When God allowed this burden
to be put upon you,
He put his arms underneath you
to help you carry it.

God's Spirit is right alongside helping us along.
If we don't know how or what to pray, it doesn't matter.
He does our praying in and for us, making prayer
out of our wordless sighs, our aching groans.
ROMANS 8:26 *The Message*

6

Lean on the God of all healing.
He walks beside you
even when you feel alone.
He is always there
when we go through hard times.
He has been there for me
and now puts you in my path
so we can take comfort together.

For he will command his angels concerning you to guard
you in all your ways; they will lift you up in their hands.
PSALM 91:11–12

*Do not look forward to the changes and chances of
this life in fear; rather look to them with full hope
that, as they arise, God, whose you are,
will deliver you out of them.
He is your keeper. He has kept you hitherto.
Do you but hold fast to His dear hand, and
He will lead you safely through all things; and when
you cannot stand, He will bear you in His arms.*

Do not look forward to what may happen tomorrow.
Our Father will either shield you from suffering,
or He will give you strength to bear it.
SAINT FRANCIS OF SALES

Even now when your heart is twisted in pain,
God is with you. Jesus, too, suffered in anguish
and cried out to His Father in heaven.
Our loving God and Father gave His only Son
the courage and strength to go on.

"Now my heart is troubled, and what shall I say?
'Father, save me from this hour'?
No, it was for this very reason I came to this hour.
JOHN 12:27

The pain is great, but greater is the Comforter.

The hurt is there to make us stronger.

God never promised us a life without sorrow.

Jesus died to take away our sins,

but He did not take away our feelings.

Our bodies are not yet transformed.

That is why they get worn out and sick,

and that is why they die.

For the perishable must clothe itself with the imperishable, and the mortal with immortality. When the perishable has been clothed with the imperishable, and the mortal with immortality, then the saying that is written will come true: "Death has been swallowed up in victory."
1 CORINTHIANS 15:53–54

Why do people keep saying, "lost"?
When told her grandpa was lost, a child said,
"Let's go find him." A child understands better
than we do. Our loved ones are not "lost."
We know they are with the Lord.
The shadow of death is thin.
Beyond it is a new life with the Savior.
He has plans for our loved ones and for us.
No one is "lost" who believes in Jesus Christ.
Don't think in terms of a "dim future"
for that loved one who has gone to be with Christ.
The future is bright!

For I know the plans I have for you, says the LORD, plans
for welfare and not for evil, to give you a future and a hope.
JEREMIAH 29:11 RSV

From the Comfort Chapter

Let not your heart be troubled: ye believe in God,
believe also in me.
In my Father's house are many mansions:
if it were not so, I would have told you.
I go to prepare a place for you.
And if I go and prepare a place for you,
I will come again, and receive you unto myself;
that where I am, there ye may be also.
If ye love me, keep my commandments.
And I will pray the Father, and he shall give you another
Comforter, that he may abide with you for ever.
Peace I leave with you, my peace I give unto you:
not as this world giveth, give I unto you.
Let not your heart be troubled,
neither let it be afraid.
JOHN 14:1–3, 15–16, 27 KJV

12

The path of grief is not easy.
Have you traveled in the mountains and looked at a
rock wall to see
a tiny bush clinging to the rocks?
This is where we are at this point.
Where the saying "hang in there" has a
real meaning. God nourishes that small plant, and
His comfort is ever with you
to nourish you on your journey.

For I am about to fall, and my pain is ever with me.
PSALM 38:17

Though I cannot share the pain you feel,
I can help you move beyond it.
I have walked the path of grief
and hold out a hand to guide you.
I can show you that good things
can still take place in spite of
the magnitude of your loss.

Those who sow in tears will reap with songs of joy.
PSALM 126:5

We know that God does not
willingly afflict us with grief.
He looks at those who grieve with pity.
He nourishes our souls with patience.
He comforts us and gives us
a sense of His mercy.
His words to Martha when her brother died bring a
sense of peace to us in our pain.

Jesus said to her, "I am the resurrection and the life.
He who believes in me will live, even though he dies;
and whoever lives and believes in me will never die.
Do you believe this?"
JOHN 11:25–26

15

Love

Love is the definition of God.
Although it is true that no one
can know exactly how you feel, may it
comfort you to know others care deeply.
Every person you meet is
fighting a difficult battle.
Let those of us who have walked
the path of grief reach out
to help you along the way.

Trust in the LORD with all your heart and lean not on your own understanding; in all your ways acknowledge him, and he will make your paths straight.

PROVERBS 3:5–6

Those of us who reach out to you do not do so
out of strength but rather from our own weakness.
We are powerless to take away your pain and hurt.
We can only break through that barrier of
your sorrow because we have suffered.
We know what despair is, and
we reach out our hands to comfort and guide you.

Almost without exception those who survive a tragedy
give credit to one person who stood by them,
supported them, and gave them a sense of hope.
ROBERT VENINGA
in *A Gift of Hope*

*A real friend will be your companion—
one you can trust never to abandon you.
Reach out to share with the one who offers hope.
A good friendship will affirm that good things
can still happen even after your tremendous loss.
Believe that person, and share your frustrations
with him or her. Accept the gift of hope.
If it weren't for hope, the heart would break.
Believe the friend who urges you to have hope and
faith that the Lord will come again.*

For he must reign until he has put all his enemies under his
feet. The last enemy to be destroyed is death.
1 CORINTHIANS 15:25–26

Be Still, My Soul

Be still, my soul: the Lord is on thy side.
Bear patiently the cross of grief or pain.
Leave to thy God to order and provide;
In every change, He faithful will remain.
Be still, my soul: thy best, thy heavenly friend
Through thorny ways leads to a joyful end.

Be still, my soul: thy God doth undertake
To guide the future, as He has the past,
Thy hope, thy confidence let nothing shake;
All now mysterious shall be bright at last.
Be still, my soul: the waves and winds shall know
His voice Who ruled them while He dwelt below.

continued on next page

continued from previous page

Be still, my soul: the hour is hastening on
When we shall be forever with the Lord.
When disappointment, grief and fear are gone,
Sorrow forgot, love's purest joys restored.
Be still, my soul: when change and tears are past
All safe and blessed we shall meet at last.

KATHARINA VON SCHLEGEL

Don't hide your sadness.
You are safe with your friends
to let the pain show.
We are here to offer a hug,
a shoulder to cry on, or an ear to listen. Share your
memories of your loved one.
It is in this sharing of memories you keep
him or her alive in your heart.

Stoop down and reach out to those who are oppressed.
Share their burdens, and so complete Christ's law.
GALATIANS 6:2 *The Message*

God's number is not *911*. Don't expect angels
to the rescue as soon as you cry out.
All things come in God's time.
That is when you must be willing to let your
imperfect friends guide you. We have suffered grief
and have grown stronger in faith because of it.
Now we are here to give you the strength to go on.
Death cannot be dismissed.
Like fear it must be faced,
but you do not have to face the specter alone.

"Hear my prayer, O LORD,
listen to my cry for help;
be not deaf to my weeping."
PSALM 39:12

Right now your life is in crisis,
but feelings of this sort are transitory.
Such emotions come and go. When they come,
a good use can be made of them.
Those of us who reach out to you have
gone through crises and learned from them.
Someday you will reach out to another who is in pain.

Dear friends, do not be surprised at the painful trial
you are suffering, as though something strange were
happening to you. But rejoice that you participate in the
sufferings of Christ, so that you may be overjoyed
when his glory is revealed.
1 PETER 4:12–13

In *God Calling* we are told only scarred lives
can really save. It is in suffering that we meet God.
It is in pain that we meet God face-to-face.
If life is only a smooth path, we do not grow.
Right now you suffer growing pains
brought on by the death of one you love.
Others have made their way through this rough
way. You, too, will be battle-scarred but victorious.

Cast your cares on the LORD and he will sustain you;
he will never let the righteous fall.
PSALM 55:22

24

Each of us carries a burden.
We can share our cares and comfort each other.
Most of all, we can pray,
not for lighter burdens but for stronger backs.
The Lord will always be there to support us.
He will sustain us and not let us fall.

My soul finds rest in God alone;
my salvation comes from him.
He alone is my rock and my salvation;
he is my fortress, I will never be shaken.
PSALM 62:1–2

*When loneliness overwhelms you and you long
to have your loved one back, remember where
he is. Would you really ask him to return
to this world when you know he is safe
with the Lord? Rather think of God's promise to us.*

The LORD is my shepherd; I shall not want.
He maketh me to lie down in green pastures:
he leadeth me beside still waters. He restoreth my soul:
he leadeth me in paths of righteousness for his name's sake.
Yea, though I walk through the valley of the shadow of
death, I will fear no evil: for thou art with me;
thy rod and thy staff they comfort me.
PSALM 23:1–4 KJV

All Thro' the Year

The world's a weary place,
For him who tries to face
His tasks alone.
But he who looks above,
Will see the God of love
Is always swift to move
Among His own.
And so I wish for thee
The vision clear to see,
A presence near;
That every hour of night
And all the days of light,
May with God's love shine bright
All thro' the year.

AUTHOR UNKNOWN

Healing

He will turn our pain into grace.
Death is an intrinsic part of life.
We know it is there, but we must not dwell on that.
We need to move on—to seek life.
It is not the load that will break you down
but the way you carry it.

Be merciful to me, LORD, for I am faint; O LORD,
heal me, for my bones are in agony.
PSALM 6:2

*The medicine we need to heal
is found in the Bible.
It is full of vitamins for a healthy soul.*

Outside of the Bible,
death forever remains an unknown phantom,
stalking helpless human victims.
BILLY GRAHAM

When you see a beautiful tapestry, it will be more than bright, vibrant colors. It is the great sorrow of human suffering, like the death of a loved one that provides the dark threads in the tapestry of life. Those dark shadows are the lines that define the pattern.

Tapestry

My life is but a weaving between God and me.
I do not choose the colors; He worketh steadily.
Oft times He weaves sorrow, and I in foolish pride,
forget He sees the upper, and I the underside.

Not 'til the loom is silent and shuttles cease to fly,
will God unroll the canvas and explain the reason why.
The dark threads are as needful in the skillful
Weaver's Hand, as the threads of gold and silver
in the pattern He has planned.

AUTHOR UNKNOWN

Cancer is not God's will.
The death of a child is not God's will.
Tragedies are consequences of human actions.
God does not cause the tragedy but lovingly comes
into the anguish with us.
MADELEINE L'ENGLE

It is natural to be angry with God.

Why did He let this happen?

Try to admit that anger and move beyond it.

When we refuse to spend time mourning a loss,

we will carry that loss the rest of our lives.

Let go of anger and allow the love of friends

to help you out of this darkness.

I saw something meaningless under the sun:
There was a man all alone; he had neither son nor brother.
There was no end to his toil,
yet his eyes were not content with his wealth.
"For whom am I toiling," he asked,
"and why am I depriving myself of enjoyment?"
ECCLESIASTES 4:7–8

Please do not toil alone on your journey.
Allow those around you to reach out with a touch,
a hug, or a word of comfort.
Let yourself feel the warmth of friendship.

"The Spirit of the Sovereign LORD is on me,
because the LORD has anointed me. . .
to comfort all who mourn."
ISAIAH 61:1–2

If we obey what God says according to our sincere belief,
God will break us from those traditions that
misrepresent Him. There are many such beliefs
to be gotten rid of, for example,
that God removes a child because the mother loves him
too much—a devil's lie!—
and a travesty of the true nature of God.
If the devil can hinder us from taking the supreme climb
and getting rid of wrong traditions about God,
he will do so; but if we keep true to God,
God will take us through an ordeal which will bring us
out into a better knowledge of Himself.
OSWALD CHAMBERS

When he was dying of cancer,
Hubert Humphrey wrote:

The greatest healing therapy is friendship and love,
and over this land I have sensed it. Doctors, chemicals,
radiation, pills, nurses, therapists—are all very helpful.
But without faith in yourself and your own ability
to overcome your own difficulties, faith in divine
providence, and with the friendship and kindness and
generosity of friends, there is no healing.

This man faced death leaving behind the prescription to
heal a broken heart. We must keep our faith but that faith
is not a promise that everything will turn out pleasantly.
Instead, faith gives us the confidence that no matter how
things turn out, God will somehow use the events
of our days for His glory and our good.

Hope

Soft as the voice, as the voice of a
Zephyr, breathing unheard,
Hope gently whispers, through the shadows,
Her comforting word:
Wait till the darkness is over,
Wait till the tempest is done,
Hope for the sunshine, hope for the morrow,
After the storm has gone.

We only grow through pain and suffering.
God is not punishing us, He is teaching us.
When He allows us sorrow, He will be there to sustain us.

You will not grow if you sit in a beautiful
flower garden and somebody brings you
gorgeous food on a silver platter.
But you will grow if you are sick,
if you are in pain, if you experience losses,
and if you do not put your head in the sand
but take the pain and learn to accept it
not as a curse, or a punishment,
but as a gift to you with a very,
very specific purpose.

ELISABETH KUBLER–ROSS

The path is painful and rough in spots,
but it will end.
You will forever carry the wounds of sorrow,
but there is life beyond this wrenching grief.
Take heart, for tomorrow will be better.

You will surely forget your trouble,
recalling it only as waters gone by.
Life will be brighter than noonday,
and darkness will become like morning.
You will be secure, because there is hope;
you will look about you and take your rest in safety.
JOB 11:16–18

Don't Quit

When things go wrong as they sometimes will,
When the road you're trudging seems all uphill,
When funds are low, and the debts are high,
And you want to smile, but you have to sigh,
When care is pressing you down a bit—
Rest if you must, but don't you quit.

Success is failure turned inside out,
The silver tint of the clouds of doubt,
And you never can tell how close you are,
It may be near when it seems far.
So, stick to the fight when you're hardest hit—
It's when things go wrong that you mustn't quit.

AUTHOR UNKNOWN

A full life will be full of pain.
But the alternative is to not live life fully
or not to live at all.

I waited patiently for the LORD; and he inclined unto me, and heard my cry. He brought me up also out of an horrible pit, out of the miry clay, and set my feet upon a rock, and established my goings. And he hath put a new song in my mouth, even praise unto our God.

PSALM 40:1–3 KJV

Be brave, my friend.
Others have walked this path before you,
and we promise you this pain won't last forever.